Enterin゛... ᴐm

CW00455594

Janice & Mel's
Life Transformation Publishing
2013

ISBN-13: 978-1484935590

ISBN-10: 1484935594

Janice & Mel's
Life Transformation Publishing
www.lifetransformationpublishing.com
2013

Specializing in Transforming Lives!

Check out our other titles at the end of the book!

CONTENTS

Foreword   4

The Soul's Great Need   5

The Competitive Laws and The Law of Love   8

The Finding of a Principle   30

At Rest in The Kingdom and All Things Added   50

Foreword

In seeking for pleasures here and rewards hereafter men have destroyed (in their hearts) the Temple of Righteousness, and have wandered from the Kingdom of Heaven. By ceasing to seek for earthly pleasures and heavenly rewards, the Temple of Righteousness is restored and the Kingdom of Heaven is found. This truth is for those who are ready to receive it; and this book also is for those whose souls have been prepared for the acceptance of its teaching.

James Allen.

The Soul's Great Need

I sought the world, but Peace was not there;
I courted learning, but Truth was not revealed;
I sojourned with philosophy, but my heart was sore
with vanity.
And I cried, Where is Peace to be found!
And where is the hiding place of truth!

Filius Lucis

EVERY HUMAN SOUL IS IN NEED. The expression of that need varies with individuals, but there is not one soul that does not feel it in some degree. It is a spiritual and casual need which takes the form, in souls of a particular development, of a deep and inexpressible hunger which the outward things of life, however abundantly they may be possessed, can never satisfy. Yet the majority, imperfect in knowledge and misled by appearances, seek to satisfy this hunger by striving for material possessions, believing that these will satisfy their need, and bring them peace.

Every soul, consciously or unconsciously, hungers for righteousness, and every soul seeks to gratify that hunger in its own particular way, and in accordance with its own particular state of knowledge. The hunger is one, and the righteousness is one, but the pathways by which righteousness is sought are many.

They who seek consciously are blessed, and shall shortly find that final and permanent satisfaction of soul which righteousness alone can give, for they have come into a knowledge of the true path.

They who seek unconsciously, although for a time they may bathe in a sea of pleasure, are not blessed, for they are carving out for themselves pathways of suffering over which they must walk with torn and wounded feet, and their hunger will increase, and the soul will cry out for its lost heritage—the eternal heritage of righteousness.

Not in any of the three worlds (waking, dream and sleep) can the soul find lasting satisfaction, apart from the realization of righteousness. Bodied or disembodied, it is ceaselessly driven on by the discipline of suffering, until at last, in its extremity, it flies to its only refuge—the refuge of righteousness—and finds that joy, satisfaction, and peace which it had so long and so vainly sought.

The great need of the soul, then, is the need of this permanent principle, called righteousness, on which it may stand securely and restfully amid the tempest of earthly existence, no more bewildered, and whereon it may build the mansion of a beautiful, peaceful, and perfect life.

It is the realization of this principle where the Kingdom of Heaven, the abiding home of the soul, resides, and which is the source and storehouse of every permanent blessing. Finding it, all is found; not finding it, all is lost. It is an attitude of mind, a state of consciousness, an ineffable knowledge, in which the struggle for existence ceases, and the soul finds itself at rest in the midst of plenty, where its great need, yea, its every need, is satisfied, without strife and without fear. Blessed are they who earnestly and intelligently seek, for it is impossible that such should seek in vain.

The Competitive Laws and the Law of Love

When I am pure
I shall have solved the mystery of life,
I shall be sure
(When I am free from hatred, lust and strife)
I am in truth, and Truth abides in me.
I shall be safe and sane and wholly free
When I am pure.

IT HAS BEEN SAID that the laws of Nature are cruel; it has likewise been said that they are kind. The one statement is the result of dwelling exclusively upon the fiercely competitive aspect of Nature; the other results from viewing only the protective and kindly aspect. In reality, natural laws are neither cruel or kind; they are absolutely just—are, in fact, the outworking of the indestructible principle of justice itself.

The cruelty, and consequent suffering, which is so prevalent in Nature, is not inherent in the heart and substance of life; it is a passing phase of evolution, a painful experience, which will ultimately ripen into the fruit of a more perfect knowledge; a dark night of ignorance and unrest, leading to a glorious morning of joy and peace.

When a helpless child is burnt to death, we do not ascribe cruelty to the working of the natural law by virtue of which the child was consumed; we infer ignorance in the child, or carelessness on the part of its guardians. Even so, men and creatures are daily being consumed in the invisible flames of passion, succumbing to the ceaseless interplay of those fiery psychic forces which, in their ignorance, they do not understand, but which they shall at last learn how to control and use to their own protection, and not, as at present, foolishly employ them to their own destruction.

To understand, control and harmoniously adjust the invisible forces of its own soul is the ultimate destiny of every being and creature. Some men and women, in the past, have accomplished this supreme and exalted purpose; some, in the present, have likewise succeeded, and, until this is done, that place of rest wherein one receives all that is necessary for one's well-being and happiness, without striving, and with freedom from pain, cannot be entered.

In an age like the present, when, in all civilized countries, the string of life is strained to its highest pitch, when men and women, striving each with each in every department of life for the vanities and material possessions of this perishable existence, have developed competition to the utmost limit of endurance—in such an age the sublimest heights of knowledge are scaled, the supremest spiritual conquests are achieved; for when the soul is most tired, its need is greatest, and where the need is great, great will be the effort. Where, also, the temptations are powerful, the greater and more enduring will be the victory.

Men love the competitive strife with their fellows, while it promises, and seems to bring them gain and happiness; but when the inevitable reaction comes, and the cold steel of selfish strife which their own hands have forged enters their own hearts, then, and not till then, do they seek a better way.

"Blessed are they that mourn,"—that have come to the end of strife, and have found the pain and sorrow to which it leads; for unto them, and unto them only, can open the door which leads to the Kingdom of Peace.

In searching for this Kingdom, it is necessary to fully understand the nature of that which prevents its realization—namely, the strife of nature, the competitive laws operative in human affairs, and the universal unrest, insecurity and fear which accompany these factors; for without such an understanding there can be no sound comprehension as to what constitutes the true and false in life, and therefore no real spiritual advancement.

Before the true can be apprehended and enjoyed, the false must be unveiled; before the real can be perceived as the real, the illusions which distort it must be dispersed; and before the limitless expanse of Truth can open before us, the limited experience which is confined to the world of visible and superficial effects must be transcended.

Let, therefore, those of my readers who are thoughtful and earnest, and who are diligently seeking, or are willing to seek, for that basis of thought and conduct which shall simplify and harmonize the bewildering complexities and inequalities of life, walk with me step by step as I open up the way to the Kingdom; first descending into Hell (the world of strife and self-seeking) in order that, having comprehended its intricate ways, we may afterwards ascend into Heaven (the world of Peace and Love).

It is the custom in my household, during the hard frosts of winter, to put out food for the birds, and it is a noticeable fact that these creatures, when they are really starving, live together most amicably, huddling together to keep each other warm, and refraining from all strife; and if a small quantity of food be given them they will eat it with comparative freedom from contention; but let a quantity of food which is more than sufficient for all be thrown to them, and fighting over the coveted supply at once ensues.

Occasionally we would put out a whole loaf of

bread, and then the contention of the birds became fierce and prolonged, although there was more than they could possibly eat during several days. Some, having gorged themselves until they could eat no more, would stand upon the loaf and hover round it, pecking fiercely at all newcomers, and endeavouring to prevent them from obtaining any of the food. And along with this fierce contention there was notice-ably a great fear. With each mouthful of food taken, the birds would look around in nervous terror, appre-hensive of losing their food or their lives.

In this simple incident we have an illustration— crude, perhaps, but true—of the basis and outwork-ing of the competitive laws in Nature and in human affairs. It is not scarcity that produces competition, it is abundance; so that the richer and more luxurious a nation becomes, the keener and fiercer becomes the competition for securing the necessaries and luxuries of life.

Let famine overtake a nation, and at once compas-sion and sympathy take the place of competitive strife; and, in the blessedness of giving and receiv-ing, men enjoy a foretaste of that heavenly bliss which the spiritually wise have found, and which all shall ultimately reach.

The fact that abundance, and not scarcity, creates competition, should be held constantly in mind by the reader during the perusal of this book, as it throws a searching light not only on the statements herein contained, but upon every problem relating to social life and human conduct. Moreover, if it be deeply and earnestly meditated upon, and its lessons applied to individual conduct, it will make plain the Way which leads to the Kingdom.

Let us now search out the cause of this fact, in order that the evils connected with it may be transcended.

Every phenomenon in social and national life (as in Nature) is an effect, and all these effects are embodied by a cause which is not remote and detached, but which is the immediate soul and life of the effect itself. As the seed is contained in the flower, and the flower in the seed, so the relation of cause and effect is intimate and inseparable. An effect also is vivified and propagated, not by any life inherent in itself, but by the life and impulse existing in the cause.

Looking out upon the world, we behold it as an arena of strife in which individuals, communities, and nations are constantly engaged in struggle, striving with each other for superiority, and for the largest share of worldly possessions.

We see, also, that the weaker fall out defeated, and that the strong — those who are equipped to pursue the combat with undiminished ardour — obtain the victory, and enter into possession. And along with this struggle we see the suffering which is inevitably connected with it — men and women, broken down with the weight of their responsibilities, failing in their efforts and losing all; families and communities broken up, and nations subdued and subordinated.

We see seas of tears, telling of unspeakable anguish and grief; we see painful partings and early and un-natural deaths; and we know that this life of strife, when stripped of its surface appearances, is largely a life of sorrow. h that aspect of human life with which we are now dealing; such are the effects as we see them; and they have one common cause which is found in the human heart itself.

As all the multiform varieties of plant life have one common soil from which to draw their sustenance, and by virtue of which they live and thrive, so all the varied activities of human life are rooted in, and draw their vitality from, one common source—the human heart. The cause of all suffering and of all happiness resides, not in the outer activities of human life, but in the inner activities of the heart and mind; and every external agency is sustained by the life which it derives from human conduct.

The organized life-principle in man carves for itself outward channels along which it can pour its pent-up energies, makes for itself vehicles through which it can manifest its potency and reap its experience, and, as a result, we have our religious, social and political organizations.

All the visible manifestations of human life, then, are effects; and as such, although they may possess a reflex action, they can never be causes, but must remain forever what they are—dead effects, galvanized into life by an enduring and profound cause.

It is the custom of men to wander about in this world of effects, and to mistake its illusions for realities, eternally transposing and readjusting these effects in order to arrive at a solution of human problems, instead of reaching down to the underlying cause which is at once the centre of unification and the basis upon which to build a peace-giving solution of human life.

The strife of the world in all its forms, whether it be war, social or political quarrelling, sectarian hatred, private disputes or commercial competition, has its origin in one common cause, namely, individual selfishness. And I employ this term selfishness in a far-reaching sense; in it I include all forms of self-love and egotism— I mean by it the desire to pander to, and preserve at all costs, the personality.

This element of selfishness is the life and soul of competition, and of the competitive laws. Apart from it they have no existence. But in the life of every individual in whose heart selfishness in any form is harboured, these laws are brought into play, and the individual is subject to them.

Innumerable economic systems have failed, and must fail, to exterminate the strife of the world. They are the outcome of the delusion that outward systems of government are the causes of that strife, whereas they are but the visible and transient effect of the inward strife, the channels through which it must necessarily manifest itself. To destroy the channel is, and must ever be ineffectual, as the inward energy will immediately make for itself another, and still another and another.

Strife cannot cease; and the competitive laws must prevail so long as selfishness is fostered in the heart. All reforms fail where this element is ignored or unaccounted for; all reforms will succeed where it is recognized, and steps are taken for its removal.

Selfishness, then, is the root cause of competition, the foundation on which all competitive systems rest, and the sustaining source of the competitive laws. It will thus be seen that all competitive systems, all the visible activities of the struggle of man with man, are as the leaves and branches of a tree which overspreads the whole earth, the root of that tree being individual selfishness, and the ripened fruits of which are pain and sorrow.

This tree cannot be destroyed by merely lopping off its branches; to do this effectively, the root must be destroyed. To introduce measures in the form of changed external conditions is merely lopping off the branches; and as the cutting away of certain branches of a tree gives added vigour to those which remain, even so the very means which are taken to curtail the competitive strife, when those means deal entirely with its outward effects, will but add strength and vigour to the tree whose roots are all the time being fostered and encouraged in the human heart. The most that even legislation can do is to prune the branches, and so prevent the tree from altogether running wild.

Great efforts are now being put forward to found a "Garden City," which shall be a veritable Eden planted in the midst of orchards, and whose inhabitants shall live in comfort and comparative repose. And beautiful and laudable are all such efforts when they are prompted by unselfish love. But such a city cannot exist, or cannot long remain the Eden which it aims to be in its outward form, unless the majority of its inhabitants have subdued and conquered the inward selfishness.

Even one form of selfishness, namely, self-indulgence, if fostered by its inhabitants, will completely undermine that city, levelling its orchards to the ground, converting many of its beautiful dwellings into competitive marts, and obnoxious centres for the personal gratification of appetite, and some of its buildings into institutions for the maintenance of order; and upon its public spaces will rise jails, asylums, and orphanages, for where the spirit of self-indulgence is, the means for its gratification will be immediately adopted, without considering the good of others or of the community (for selfishness is always blind), and the fruits of that gratification will be rapidly reaped.

The building of pleasant houses and the planting of beautiful gardens can never, of itself, constitute a Garden City unless its inhabitants have learned that self-sacrifice is better than self-protection, and have first established in their own hearts the Garden City of unselfish love. And when a sufficient number of men and women have done this, the Garden City will appear, and it will flourish and prosper, and great will be its peace, for "out of the heart are the issues of life."

Having found that selfishness is the root cause of all competition and strife, the question naturally arises as to how this cause shall be dealt with, for it natu-rally follows that a cause being destroyed, all its ef-fects cease; a cause being propagated, all its effects, however they may be modified from without, must continue.

Every man who has thought at all deeply upon the problem of life, and has brooded sympathetically upon the sufferings of mankind, has seen that selfishness is at the root of all sorrow—in fact, this is one of the truths that is first apprehended by the thoughtful mind. And along with that perception there has been born within him a longing to formulate some methods by which that selfishness might be overcome.

The first impulse of such a man is to endeavour to frame some outward law, or introduce some new social arrangements or regulations, which shall put a check on the selfishness of others.

The second tendency of his mind will be to feel his utter helplessness before the great iron will of selfishness by which he is confronted.

Both these attitudes of mind are the result of an incomplete knowledge of what constitutes selfishness. And this partial knowledge dominates him because, although he has overcome the grosser forms of selfishness in himself, and is so far noble, he is yet selfish in other and more remote and subtle directions.

This feeling of "helplessness" is the prelude to one of two conditions—the man will either give up in despair, and again sink himself in the selfishness of the world, or he will search and meditate until he finds another way out of the difficulty. And that way he will find. Looking deeper and ever deeper into the things of life; reflecting, brooding, examining, and analysing; grappling with every difficulty and problem with intensity of thought, and developing day by day a profounder love of Truth—by these means his heart will grow and his comprehension expand, and at last he will realize that the way to destroy selfishness is not to try to destroy one form of it in other people, but to destroy it utterly, root and branch, in himself.

The perception of this truth constitutes spiritual illumination, and when once it is awakened in the mind, the "straight and narrow way" is revealed, and the Gates of the Kingdom already loom in the distance.

Then does a man apply to himself (not to others) these words—And why beholdest thou the mote that is in thy brother's eye, but considerest not the beam that is in thy own eye? Or how wilt thou say to thy brother, let me pull out the mote out of thine eye; and, behold, a beam is in thine own eye? Thou hypocrite, first cast out the beam out of thine own eye; and then shall thou see clearly to cast out the mote out of thine brother's eye.

When a man can apply these words to himself and

act upon them, judging himself mercilessly, but judging none other, then will he find his way out of the hell of competitive strife, then will he rise above and render of non-effect the laws of competition, and will find the higher Law of Love, subjecting himself to which every evil thing will flee from him, and the joys and blessings which the selfish vainly seek will constantly wait upon him. And not only this, he will, having lifted himself, lift the world. By his example many will see the Way, and will walk it; and the powers of darkness will be weaker for having lived.

It will here be asked, "But will not man who has risen above his selfishness, and therefore above the competitive strife, suffer through the selfishness and competition of those around him? Will he not after all the trouble he has taken to purify himself, suffer at the hands of the impure?"

No, he will not. The equity of the Divine Order is perfect, and cannot be subverted, so that it is impossible for one who has overcome selfishness to be subject to those laws which are brought into operation by the action of selfishness; in other words, each individual suffers by virtue of his own selfishness.

It is true that the selfish all come under the operation of the competitive laws, and suffer collectively, each acting, more or less, as the instrument by which the suffering of others is brought about, which makes it appear, on the surface, as though men suffered for the sins of others rather than their own. But the truth is that in a universe the very basis of which is harmony, and which can only be sustained by the perfect adjustment of all its parts, each unit receives its own measure of adjustment, and suffers by and of itself.

Each man comes under the laws of his own being, never under those of another. True, he will suffer like another, and even through the instrumentality of another, if he elects to live under the same conditions as that other. But if he chooses to desert those conditions and to live under another and higher set of conditions of which that other is ignorant, he will cease to come under, or be affected by, the lower laws.

Let us now go back to the symbol of the tree and carry the analogy a little further. Just as the leaves and branches are sustained by the roots, so the roots derive their nourishment from the soil, groping blindly in the darkness for the sustenance which the tree demands. In like manner, selfishness, the root of the tree of evil and of suffering, derives its nourishment from the dark soil of ignorance. In this it thrives; upon this it stands and flourishes. By ignorance I mean something vastly different from lack of learning; and the sense in which I use it will be made plain as I proceed.

Selfishness always gropes in the dark. It has no knowledge; by its very nature it is cut off from the source of enlightenment; it is a blind impulse, knowing nothing, obeying no law, for it knows none, and is thereby forcibly bound to those competitive laws by virtue of which suffering is inflicted in order that harmony may be maintained.

We live in a world, a universe, abounding with all good things. So great is the abundance of spiritual, mental and material blessings that every man and woman on this globe could not only be provided with every necessary good, but could live in the midst of abounding plenty, and yet have much to spare. Yet, in spite of this, what a spectacle of ignorance do we behold!

We see on the one hand millions of men and women chained to a ceaseless slavery, interminably toiling in order to obtain a poor and scanty meal and a garment to cover their nakedness; and on the other hand we see thousands, who already have more than they require and can well manage, depriving themselves of all the blessings of a true life and of the vast opportunities which their possessions place within their reach, in order to accumulate more of those material things for which they have no legitimate use. Surely men and women have no more wisdom than the beasts which fight over the possession of that which is more than they can all well dispose of, and which they could all enjoy in peace!

Such a condition of things can only occur in a state of ignorance deep and dark; so dark and dense as to be utterly impenetrable save to the unselfish eye of wisdom and truth. And in the midst of all this striving after place and food and raiment, there works unseen, yet potent and unerring, the Overruling Law of Justice, meting out to every individual his own quota of merit and demerit. It is impartial; it bestows no favours; it inflicts no unearned punishments:

It knows not wrath nor pardon; utter-true
It measures mete, its faultless balance weighs;
Times are as nought, tomorrow it will judge,
Or after many days.

The rich and the poor alike suffer for their own selfishness; and none escapes. The rich have their particular sufferings as well as the poor. Moreover, the rich are continually losing their riches; the poor are continually acquiring them. The poor man of today is the rich man of tomorrow, and vice versa.

There is no stability, no security in hell, and only brief and occasional periods of respite from suffering in some form or other. Fear, also, follows men like a great shadow, for the man who obtains and holds by selfish force will always be haunted by a feeling of insecurity, and will continually fear its loss; while the poor man, who is selfishly seeking or coveting material riches, will be harassed by the fear of destitution. And one and all who live in this underworld of strife are overshadowed by one great fear—the fear of death.

Surrounded by the darkness of ignorance, and having no knowledge of those eternal and life-sustaining Principles out of which all things proceed, men labour under the delusion that the most important and essential things in life are food and clothing, and that their first duty is to strive to obtain these, believing that these outward things are the source and cause of all comfort and happiness.

It is the blind animal instinct of self-preservation (the preservation of the body and personality), by virtue of which each man opposes himself to other men in order to "get a living" or "secure a competency," believing that if he does not keep an incessant watch on other men, and constantly renew the struggle, they will ultimately "take the bread out of his mouth."

It is out of this initial delusion that comes all the train of delusions, with their attendant sufferings. Food and clothing are not the essential things of life; not the causes of happiness. They are non-essentials, effects, and, as such, proceed by a process of natural law from the essentials, the underlying cause.

The essential things in life are the enduring elements in character—integrity, faith, righteousness, self-sacrifice, compassion, love; and out of these all good things proceed.

Food and clothing, and money are dead effects; there is in them no life, no power except that which we invest with them. They are without vice and virtue, and can neither bless nor harm. Even the body which men believe to be themselves, to which they pander, and which they long to keep, must very shortly be yielded up to the dust. But the higher elements of character are life itself; and to practice these, to trust them, and to live entirely in them, constitutes the Kingdom of Heaven.

The man who says, "I will first of all earn a competence and secure a good position in life, and will then give my mind to those higher things," does not understand these higher things, does not believe them to be higher, for if he did, it would not be possible for him to neglect them. He believes the material outgrowths of life to be the higher, and therefore he seeks them first. He believes money, clothing and position to be of vast and essential importance, righteousness and truth to be at best secondary; for a man always sacrifices that which he believes to be lesser to that which he believes to be greater.

Immediately after a man realizes that righteousness is of more importance than the getting of food and clothing, he ceases to strive after the latter, and begins to live for the former. It is here where we come to the dividing line between the two Kingdoms— Hell and Heaven.

Once a man perceives the beauty and enduring reality of righteousness, his whole attitude of mind toward himself and others and the things within and around him changes. The love of personal existence gradually loses its hold on him; the instinct of self-preservation begins to die, and the practice of self-renunciation takes its place. For the sacrifice of others, or of the happiness of others, for his own good, he substitutes the sacrifice of self and of his own happiness for the good of others. And thus, rising above self, he rises above the competitive strife which is the outcome of self, and above the competitive laws which operate only in the region of self, and for the regulation of its blind impulses.

He is like the man who has climbed a mountain, and thereby risen above all the disturbing currents in the valleys below him. The clouds pour down their rain, the thunders roll and the lightnings flash, the fogs obscure, and the hurricanes uproot and destroy, but they cannot reach him on the calm heights where he stands, and where he dwells in continual sunshine and peace.

In the life of such a man the lower laws cease to operate, and he now comes under the protection of a higher Law—namely, the Law of Love; and, in accordance with his faithfulness and obedience to this Law, will all that is necessary for his well-being come to him at the time when he requires it.

The idea of gaining a position in the world cannot enter his mind, and the external necessities of life, such as money, food and clothing, he scarcely ever thinks about. But, subjecting himself for the good of others, performing all his duties scrupulously and without thinking of reward, and living day by day in the discipline of righteousness, all other things follow at the right time and in the right order.

Just as suffering and strife inhere in, and spring from, their root cause, selfishness, so blessedness and peace inhere in, and spring from, their root-cause, righteousness. And it is a full and all-embracing blessedness, complete and perfect in every department of life, for that which is morally and spiritually right is physically and materially right.

Such a man is free, for he is freed from all anxiety, worry, fear, despondency, all those mental disturbances which derive their vitality from the elements of self, and he lives in constant joy and peace, and this while living in the very midst of the competitive strife of the world.

Yet, though walking in the midst of Hell, its flames fall back before and around him, so that not one hair of his head can be singed. Though he walks in the midst of the lions of selfish force, for him their jaws are closed and their ferocity is subdued. Though on every hand men are falling around him in the fierce battle of life, he falls not, neither is he dismayed, for no deadly bullet can reach him, no poisoned shaft can pierce the impenetrable armour of his righteousness. Having lost the little, personal, self-seeking life of suffering, anxiety, fear, and want, he has found the illimitable, glorious, self-perfecting life of joy and peace and plenty.

"Therefore take no thought, saying 'What shall we eat?' or, 'What shall we drink?' or, 'Wherewithal shall we be clothed? . . .' For your heavenly Father knoweth ye have need of all these things. But seek ye first the Kingdom of God, and His Righteousness, and all these things shall be added unto you."

The Finding of a Principle

Be still, my soul, and know that peace is within
Be steadfast, heart, and know that strength divine
Belongs to thee; cease thy turmoil, mind,
And thou the everlasting rest shall find.

HOW THEN SHALL A MAN reach the Kingdom? By what process shall he find the light which alone can disperse his darkness? And in what way can he overcome the inward selfishness which is strong, and deeply rooted?

A man will reach the Kingdom by purifying himself, and he can only do this by pursuing a process of self-examination and self-analysis. The selfishness must be discovered and understood before it can be removed. It is powerless to remove itself, neither will it pass away of itself.

Darkness ceases only when light is introduced; so ignorance can only be dispersed by Knowledge; selfishness by Love. Seeing that in selfishness there is no security, no stability, no peace, the whole process of seeking the Kingdom resolves itself into a search for a Principle; a divine and permanent Principle on which a man can stand secure, freed from himself— that is, from the personal element, and from the tyranny and slavery which that personal self exacts and demands.

A man must first of all be willing to lose himself
(his self-seeking self) before he can find himself
(his Divine Self). He must realize that selfishness is
not worth clinging to, that it is a master altogether
unworthy of his service, and that divine Goodness
alone is worthy to be enthroned in his heart as the
supreme master of his life.

This means that he must have faith, for without this
equipment there can be neither progress nor achievement. He must believe in the desirability of purity,
in the supremacy of righteousness, in the sustaining
power of integrity; he must ever hold before him
the Ideal and Perfect Goodness, and strive for its
achievement with ever-renewed effort and unflag-
ging zeal.

This faith must be nurtured and its development
encouraged. As a lamp, it must be carefully trimmed
and fed and kept burning in the heart, for without its
radiating flame no way will be seen in the darkness;
he will find no pathway out of self. And as this flame
increases and burns with a steadier light, energy,
resolution, and self-reliance will come to his aid, and
with each step, his progress will be accelerated until
at last the Light of Knowledge will begin to take
the place of the lamp of faith, and the darkness will
commence to disappear before its searching splendour.

Into his spiritual sight will come the Principles of the divine Life, and as he approaches them, their incomparable beauty and majestic symmetry will astonish his vision, and gladden his heart with a gladness hitherto unknown.

Along this pathway of self-control and self-purification (for such it is) every soul must travel on its way to the Kingdom. So narrow is this way, and so overgrown with the weeds of selfishness is its entrance, that it is difficult to find, and, being found, cannot be retained except by daily meditation. Without this the spiritual energies grow weaker, and the man loses the strength necessary to continue. As the body is sustained and invigourated by material food, so the spirit is strengthened and renewed by its own food—namely meditation upon spiritual things.

He, then, who earnestly resolves to find the Kingdom will commence to meditate, and to rigidly examine his heart and mind and life in the light of that Supreme Perfection which is the goal of his attainment.

On his way to that goal, he must pass through three Gateways of Surrender. The first is the Surrender of Desire; the second is the Surrender of Opinion; the third is the Surrender of Self. Entering into meditation, he will commence to examine his desires, tracing them out in his mind, and following up their effects in his life and upon his character; and he will quickly perceive that, without the renunciation of desire, a man remains a slave both to himself and to his surroundings and circumstances. Having discovered this, the first Gate, that of the Surrender of Desire, is entered. Passing through this Gate, he adopts a process of self-discipline which is the first step in the purification of the soul.

Hitherto he has lived as a slavish beast; eating, drinking, sleeping, and pursuing enjoyment at the beck and call of his lower impulses; blindly following and gratifying his inclinations without method, not questioning his conduct, and having no fixed centre from which to regulate his character and life.

Now, however, he begins to live as a man; he curbs his inclinations, controls his passions, and steadies his mind in the practice of virtue. He ceases to pursue enjoyment, but follows the dictates of his reason, and regulates his conduct in accordance with the demands of an ideal. With the introduction of this regulating factor in his life, he at once perceives that certain habits must be abandoned.

He begins to select his food, and to have his meals at stated periods, no longer eating at any time when the sight of food tempts his inclination. He reduces the number of meals per day and also the quantity of food eaten.

He no longer goes to bed, by day or night, to indulge in pleasurable indolence, but to give his body the rest it needs, and he therefore regulates his hours of sleep, rising early, and never encouraging the animal desire to indulge in dreamy indolence after waking.

All those foods and drinks which are particularly associated with gluttony, cruelty, and drunkenness he will dispense with altogether, selecting the mild and refreshing sustenance which Nature provides in such rich profusion.

These preliminary steps will be at once adopted; and as the path of self-government and self-examination is pursued, a clearer and ever clearer perception of the nature, meaning, and effects of desire will be developed, until it will be seen that the mere regulation of one's desires is altogether inadequate and insufficient, and that the desires themselves must be abandoned, must be allowed to fall out of the mind and to have no part hi the character and life.

It is at this point where the soul of the seeker will enter the dark Valley of Temptation, for these desires will not die without a struggle, and without many a fierce effort to reassert the power and authority with which they have hitherto been invested. And here the lamp of faith must be constantly fed and assiduously trimmed, for all the light that it can throw out will be required to guide and encourage the traveller in the dense gloom of this dark Valley.

At first his desires, like so many wild beasts, will clamour loudly for gratification. Failing in that, they will tempt him to struggle with them that they may overthrow him. And this last temptation is greater and more difficult to overcome than the first, for the desires will not be stilled until they are utterly ignored; until they are left unheeded, unconditionally abandoned, and allowed to perish for want of food.

In passing through this Valley, the searcher will develop certain powers which are necessary to his further development, and these powers are—self-control, self-reliance, fearlessness, and independence of thought.

Here also he will have to pass through ridicule and mockery and false accusation; so much so, that some of his best friends, yea, even those whom he most unselfishly loves, will accuse him of folly and inconsistency, and will do all they can to argue him back to the life of animal indulgence, self-seeking, and petty personal strife.

Nearly everybody around him will suddenly discover that they know his duty better than he knows it himself, and, knowing no other and higher life than their own of mingled excitement and suffering, they will take great pains to win him back to it, imagining, in their ignorance, that he is losing so much pleasure and happiness, and is gaining nothing in return.

At first this attitude of others toward him will arouse in him acute suffering; but he will rapidly discover that this suffering is caused by his own vanity and selfishness, and is the result of his own subtle desire to be appreciated, admired, and thought well of; and immediately this knowledge is arrived at, he will rise into a higher state of consciousness, where these things can no longer reach him and inflict pain. It is here where he will begin to stand firm, and to wield with effect the powers of mind already mentioned.

Let him therefore press on courageously, heeding neither the revilings of his friends without nor the clamourings of his enemies within; aspiring, searching, striving; looking ever toward his Ideal with eyes of holy love; day by day ridding his mind of selfish motive, his heart of impure desire; stumbling sometimes, sometimes falling, but ever travelling onward and rising higher; and, recording each night in the silence of his own heart the journey of the day, let him not despair if but each day, in spite of all its failures and falls, record some holy battle fought, though lost, some silent victory attempted, though unachieved. The loss of today will add to the gain of tomorrow for him whose mind is set on the conquest of self.

Passing along the Valley, he will at last come to the Fields of Sorrow and Loneliness. His desires, having received at his hands neither encouragement nor sustenance, have grown weak, and are now falling away and perishing. He is climbing out of the Valley, and the darkness is less dense; but now he realizes for the first time he is alone. He is like a man standing upon the lowest level of a great mountain, and it is night. Above him towers the lofty peak, beyond which shine the everlasting stars; a short distance below him are the glaring lights of the city which he has left, and from it there come up to him the noises of its inhabitants—a confused mingling of shouts, screams, laughter, rumblings of traffic, and the strains of music. He thinks of his friends, all of whom are in the city, pursuing their own particular pleasures, and he is alone upon the mountain.

That city is the City of Desire and Pleasure, the mountain is the Mountain of Renunciation, and the climber now knows that he has left the world, that henceforth for him its excitements and strifes are lifeless things, and can tempt him no more. Resting awhile in this lonely place, he will taste of sorrow and learn its secret; harshness and hatred will pass from him; his heart will grow soft, and the first faint broodings of that divine compassion, which shall afterwards absorb his whole being, will overshadow and inspire him. He will begin to feel with every living thing in its strivings and sufferings, and gradually, as this lesson is learned, his own sorrow and loneliness will be forgotten in his great calm love for others, and will pass away.

Here, also, he will begin to perceive and understand the workings of those hidden laws which govern the destinies of individuals and nations. Having risen above the lower region of strife and selfishness within himself, he can now look calmly down upon it in others and in the world, and analyse and comprehend it, and he will see how selfish striving is at the root of all the world's suffering.

His whole attitude toward others and the world now undergoes a complete change, and compassion and love begin to take the place of self-seeking and self-protection in his mind; and as a result of this, the world alters in its attitude toward him.

At this juncture he perceives the folly of competition, and, ceasing from striving to overtop and get the better of others, he begins to encourage them, both with unselfish thoughts, and, when necessary, with loving acts; and this he does even to those who selfishly compete with him, no longer defending himself against them.

As a direct result of this, his worldly affairs begin to

prosper as never before; many of his friends who at first mocked him commence to respect, and even to love him, and he suddenly wakes up to the fact that he is coming in contact with people of a distinctly unworldly and noble type, of whose existence he had no knowledge while living in his lower selfish nature. From many parts and from long distances these people will come to him to minister to him and that he may minister to them, spiritual fellowship and loving brotherhood will become potent in his life, and so he will pass beyond the Fields of Sorrow and Loneliness.

The lower competitive laws have now ceased to operate in his life, and their results, which are failure, disaster, exposure, and destitution, can no longer enter into and form part of his experience; and this not merely because he has risen above the lower forms of selfishness in himself, but because also, in so rising, he has developed certain power of mind by which he is enabled to direct and govern his affairs with a more powerful and masterly hand.

He, however, has not yet travelled far, and unless he exercises constant watchfulness, may at any time fall back into the lower world of darkness and strife, revivifying its empty pleasures and galvanizing back to life its dead desires. And especially is there danger when he reaches the greatest temptation through which man is called to pass— the temptation of doubt.

Before reaching, or even perceiving, the second Gate, that of Surrender of Opinion, the pilgrim will come upon a great soul-desert, the Desert of Doubt. And here for a time he will wander around, and despondency, indecision, and uncertainty, a melancholy brood, will surround him like a cloud, hiding from his view the way immediately in front of him.

A new and strange fear, too, will possibly overtake him, and he will begin to question the wisdom of the course he is pursuing. Again the allurements of the world will be presented to him, dressed in their most attractive garb, and the drowning din and stimulating excitement of worldly battle will once more assume a desirable aspect.

"After all, am I right? What gain is there in this? Does not life itself consist of pleasure and excitement and battle, and in giving these up am I not giving up all? Am I not sacrificing the very substance of life for a meaningless shadow? May it not be that, after all, I am a poor deluded fool, and that all these around me who live the life of the senses and stand upon its solid, sure, and easily procured enjoyments are wiser than I?"

By such dark doubtings and questionings will he here be tempted and troubled, and these very doubts will drive him to a deeper searching into the intricacies of life, and arouse within him the feeling of necessity for some permanent Principle upon which to stand and take refuge.

He will therefore, while wandering about in this dark Desert, come into contact with the higher and more subtle delusions of his own mind, the delusions of the intellect; and, by contrasting these with his Ideal, will learn to distinguish between the real and the unreal, the shadow and the substance, between effect and cause, between fleeting appearances and permanent Principles.

In the Desert of Doubt a man is confronted with all forms of illusion, not only the illusions of the senses, but also those of abstract thought and religious emotion. It is in the testing of, grappling with, and ultimately destroying, these illusions that he develops still higher powers, those of discrimination, spiritual perception, steadfastness of purpose, and calmness of mind, by the exercise of which he is enabled to unerringly distinguish the true from the false, both in the world of thought and that of material appearances.

Having acquired these powers, and learned how to use them in his holy warfare as weapons against himself, he now emerges from the Desert of Doubt, the mists and mirages of delusion vanish from his pathway, and there looms before him the second Gate, the Gateway of the Surrender of Opinion.

As he approaches this Gate, he sees before him the whole pathway along which he is travelling, and, for a space, obtains a glimpse of the glorious heights of attainment toward which he is moving; he sees the Temple of the Higher Life in all its majesty, and already he feels within him the strength and joy and peace of conquest. With Sir Galahad he can now exclaim:

"I....saw the Grail,
The Holy Grail...
....And one will crown me king
Far in the spiritual city."
for he knows that his ultimate victory is assured.

He now enters upon a process of self-conquest, which is altogether distinct from that which he has hitherto pursued. Up to the present he has been overcoming, transmuting, and simplifying his ani- mal desires; now he commences to transmute and simplify his intellect. He has, so far, been adjusting his feelings to his Ideals; he now begins to adjust his thoughts to that Ideal, which also assumes at this point larger and more beautiful proportions, and for the first time he perceives what really constitutes a permanent and imperishable Principle.

He sees that the righteousness for which he has been searching is fixed and invariable; that it cannot be accommodated to man, but that man must reach up to, and obey it; that it consists of an undeviating line of conduct, apart from all considerations of loss or gain, of reward of punishment; that, in reality, it consists in abandoning self, with all the sins of desire, opinion, and self-interest of which that self is composed, and in living the blameless life of perfect love toward all men and creatures. Such a life is fixed and perfect; it is without turning, change, or qualification, and demands a sinless and perfect conduct. It is, therefore, the direct antithesis of the worldly life of self.

Perceiving this, the seeker sees that, although he has freed himself from the baser passions and desires which enslave mankind, he is still in bondage to the fetters of opinion; that although he has purified himself with a purity to which few aspire, and which the world cannot understand, he is still defiled with a defilement which is difficult to wash away—he loves his own opinions, and has all along been confounding them with Truth, with the Principle for which he is seeking.

He is not yet free from strife, and is still involved in the competitive laws as they occur in the higher realm of thought. He still believes that he (in his opinions) is right, and that others are wrong; and in his egotism, has even fallen so low as to bestow a mock pity on those who hold opinions the reverse of his own. But now, realizing this more subtle form of selfishness with which he is enslaved, and perceiving all the train of sufferings which spring from it, having also acquired the priceless possession of spiritual discernment, he reverently bends his head and passes through the second Gateway toward his final peace.

And now, clothing his soul with the colourless Garment of Humility, he bends all his energies to the uprooting of those opinions which he has hitherto loved and cherished.

He now learns to distinguish between Truth, which is one and unchangeable, and his own and others' opinions about Truth, which are many and changeable.

He sees that his opinions about Goodness, Purity, Compassion, and Love are very distinct from those qualities themselves, and that he must stand upon those divine Principles, and not upon his opinions. Hitherto he has regarded his own opinions as of great value, and the opinions of others as worthless, but now he ceases to so elevate his own opinions and to defend them against those of others, and comes to regard them as utterly worthless.

As a direct result of this attitude of mind, he takes refuge in the practice of pure Goodness, unalloyed with base desire and subtle self-love, and takes his stand upon the divine Principles of Purity, Wisdom, Compassion, and Love, incorporating them into his mind, and manifesting them in his life.

He is now clothed with the Righteousness of Christ (which is incomprehensible to the world) and is rapidly becoming divine. He has not only realized the darkness of desire; he has also perceived the vanity of speculative philosophy, and so rids his mind of all those metaphysical subtleties which have no relation to practical holiness, and which hitherto encumbered his progress and prevented him from seeing the enduring realities in life.

And now he casts from him, one after another, his opinions and speculations, and commences to live the life of perfect love toward all beings. With each opinion overcome and abandoned as a burden, there is an increased lightness of spirit, and he now begins to realize the meaning of being "free."

The divine flowers of Gladness, Joy, and Peace spring up spontaneously in his heart, and his life becomes a blissful song. And as the melody in his heart expands, and grows more and more perfect, his outward life harmonizes itself with the inward music.

All the effort he puts forth being now free from strife, he obtains all that is necessary for his well-being, without pain, anxiety, or fear. He has almost entirely transcended the competitive laws, and the Law of Love is now the governing factor in his life, adjusting all his worldly affairs harmoniously, and without struggle or difficulty on his part.

Indeed, the competitive laws as they occur in the commercial world, have been long left behind, and have ceased to touch him at any point in his material affairs. Here, also, he enters into a wider and more comprehensive consciousness, and viewing the universe and humanity from the higher altitudes of purity and knowledge to which he has ascended, perceives the orderly sequence of law in all human affairs.

The pursuit of this Path brings about the development of still higher powers of mind, and these powers are—divine patience, spiritual equanimity, non-resistance, and prophetic insight. By prophetic insight I do not mean, the foretelling of events, but direct perception of those hidden causes which operate in human life, and, indeed, in all life, and out of which spring the multifarious and universal effects and events.

The man here rises above the competitive laws as they operate in the thought world, so that their re-

sults, which are violence, ignominy, grief, humili-
ation and distress and anxiety in all their forms, no
longer occur in his life.

As he proceeds, the imperishable Principles which
form the foundation and fabric of the universe loom
before him, and assume more and more symmetrical
proportions. For him there is no more anguish; no
evil can come near his dwelling; and there breaks
upon him the dawning of the abiding Peace.

But he is not yet free. He has not yet finished his
journey. He may rest here, and that as long as he
chooses; but sooner or later he will rouse himself
to the last effort, and will reach the final goal of
achievement—the selfless state, the divine life.

He is not yet free from self, but still clings, though
with less tenacity, to the love of personal existence,
and to the idea of exclusive interest in his personal
possessions. And when he at last realizes that those
selfish elements must also be abandoned, there ap-
pears before him the third Gate—the Gateway of
Surrender of Self.

It is no dark portal which he now approaches, but
one luminous with divine glory, one radiant with a
radiance with which no earthly splendour can vie,
and he advances toward it with no uncertain step.
The clouds of Doubt have long been dispersed; the

sounds of the voices of Temptation are lost in the valley below; and with firm gait, erect carriage, and a heart filled with unspeakable joy, he nears the Gate that guards the Kingdom of God.

He has now given up all but self-interest in those things which are his by legal right, but he now perceives that he must hold nothing as his own; and as he pauses at the Gate, he hears the command which cannot be evaded or denied: "Yet lackest thou one thing; sell all that thou hast, and distribute unto the poor, and thou shall have treasure in Heaven."

And passing through the last great Gate, he stands glorious, radiant, free, detached from the tyranny of desire, of opinion, of self; a divine man—harmless, patient, tender, pure; he has found that for which he had been searching—the Kingdom of God and His Righteousness.

The journey to the Kingdom may be a long and tedious one, or it may be short and rapid. It may occupy a minute, or it may take a thousand ages. Everything depends on the faith and belief of the searcher. The majority cannot "enter in because of their unbelief"; for how can men realize righteousness when they do not believe in it nor in the possibility of its accomplishment?

Neither is it necessary to leave the outer world,

and one's duties therein. Nay, it can only be found through the unselfish performance of one's duty. Some there are whose faith is so great that, when this truth is presented to them, they can let all the personal elements drop almost immediately out of their minds, and enter into their divine heritage.

But all who believe and aspire to achieve will sooner or later arrive at victory if, amid all their worldly duties, they faint not, nor lose sight of the Ideal Goodness, and continue, with unshaken resolve to "press on to Perfection."

At Rest in the Kingdom and All Things Added

THE WHOLE JOURNEY from the Kingdom of
Strife to the Kingdom of Love resolves itself into a
process which may be summed up in the following
words: The regulation and purification of conduct.
Such a process must, if assiduously pursued, necessarily lead to perfection. It will also be seen that
as the man obtains the mastery over certain forces
within himself, he arrives at a knowledge of all the
laws which operate in the realm of those forces, and
by watching the ceaseless working of cause and effect within himself, until he understands it, he then
understands it in its universal adjustments in the
body of humanity.

Moreover, seeing that all the laws which govern
human affairs are the direct outcome of the necessities of the human heart, he, having reformed and
transmuted those necessities, has brought himself
under the guidance of other laws which operate in
accordance with the altered condition, and that, having mastered and overcome the selfish forces within
himself, he can no longer be subject to the laws
which exist for their governance.

The process is also one of simplification of the mind,
a sifting away of all but the essential gold in character. And as the mind is thus simplified, the apparent-
ly unfathomable complexity of the universe assumes

simpler and simpler aspects, until the whole is seen to resolve itself into, and rest upon, a few unalterable Principles; and these Principles are ultimately seen to be contained in one, namely LOVE.

The mind thus simplified, the man arrives at peace, and he now really begins to live. Looking back on the personal life which he has forever abandoned, he sees it as a horrible nightmare out of which he has awakened; but looking out and down with the eyes of the spirit, he sees that others continue to live it. He sees men and women struggling, fighting, suffering and perishing for that which is abundantly given to them by the bountiful hand of the Father, if they would only cease from all covetousness, and take it without hurt or hindrance; and compassion fills his heart, and also gladness, for he knows that humanity will wake at last from its long and painful dream.

In the early part of the journey he seemed to be leaving humanity far behind, and he sorrowed in his loneliness. But now, having reached the highest, having attained the goal, he finds himself nearer to humanity than ever before—yea, living in its very heart, sympathizing with all its sorrows, rejoicing in all its joys; for, having no longer any personal considerations to defend, he lives entirely in the heart of humanity.

He lives no longer for himself; he lives for others;

and so living, he enjoys the highest bliss, the deepest peace.

For a time he searched for Compassion, Love, Bliss, Truth; but now he has verily become Compassion, Love, Bliss, Truth; and it may literally be said of him that he has ceased to be a personality, for all the personal elements have been extinguished, and there remain only those qualities and principles which are entirely impersonal. And those qualities are now manifested in the man's life, and henceforth the man's character.

And having ceased from the protection of the self, and living constantly in compassion, wisdom and love, he comes under the protection of the highest Law, the Law of Love; and he understands that Law, and consciously co-operates with it; yea, is himself inseparably identified with the Law.

"Forgoing self, the universe grows I": and he whose nature is compassion, wisdom and love cannot possibly need any protection; for those Principles themselves constitute the highest protection, being the real, the divine, the immortal in all men and women, and constituting the indestructible reality in the cosmic order.

Neither does he need to seek enjoyment whose very nature is Bliss, Joy, Peace. As for competing with others, with whom should he compete who has lovingly identified himself with all? With whom should he struggle who has sacrificed himself for all? Whose blind, misguided, and ineffectual competition should he fear who has reached the source of all blessedness, and who receives at the hands of the Father all necessary things?

Having lost himself (his selfish personality), he has found himself (his divine nature, Love); and Love and all the effects of Love now compose his life. He can now joyfully exclaim—

I have made the acquaintance of the Master of Compassion;
I have put on the Garment of the Perfect Law,
I have entered the realm of the Great Reality;
Wandering is ended, for Rest is accomplished;
Pain and sorrow have ceased, for Peace is entered into;
Confusion is dissolved, for Unity is made manifest;
Error is vanquished, for Truth is revealed!

The Harmonizing Principle, Righteousness, or Divine Love, being found, all things are seen as they are, and not through the illusory mediums of selfishness and opinion; the universe is One, and all its manifold operations are the manifestation of one Law.

Hitherto in this work laws have been referred to, and also spoken of as higher and lower, and this distinction was necessary; but now the Kingdom is reached, we see that all the forces operative in human life are the varied manifestations of the One Supreme Law of Love. It is by virtue of this Law that Humanity suffers, that, by the intensity of its sufferings, it shall become purified and wise, and so relinquish the source of suffering, which is selfishness.

The Law and foundation of the universe being Love, it follows that all self-seeking is opposed to that Law, is an effort to overcome or ignore the Law, and as a result, every self-seeking act and thought is followed by an exact quota of suffering which is required to annul its effect, and so maintain the universal harmony. All suffering is, therefore, the restraint which the Law of Love puts upon ignorance and selfishness, and out of such painful restraint Wisdom at last emerges.

There being no strife and no selfishness in the Kingdom, there is therefore no suffering, no restraint; there is perfect harmony, equipoise, rest. Those who have entered it do not follow any animal inclinations (they have none to follow), but live in accordance with the highest Wisdom. Their nature is Love, and they live in love toward all.

They are never troubled about "making a living," as they are Life itself, living in the very Heart of Life; and should any material or other need arise, that need is immediately supplied without any anxiety or struggle on their part.

Should they be called to undertake any work, the money and friends needed to carry out that work are immediately forthcoming. Having ceased to violate their principles, all their needs are supplied through legitimate channels. Any money or help required always comes through the instrumentality of good people who are either living in the Kingdom themselves, or are working for its accomplishment.

Those who live in the Kingdom of Love have all their needs supplied by the Law of Love, with all freedom from unrest, just as those who live in the kingdom of self only meet their needs by much strife and suffering. Having altered the root cause in their heart they have altered all the effects in their inner and outer life. As self is the root cause of all strife and suffering, so Love is the root cause of all peace and bliss.

Those who are at rest in the Kingdom do not look for happiness to any outward possession. They see that all such possessions are mere transient effects that come when they are required, and after their purpose is served, pass away.

They never think of these things (money, clothing, food, etc.) except as mere accessories and effects of the true Life. They are therefore freed from all anxiety and trouble, and resting in Love, they are the embodiment of happiness.

Standing upon the imperishable Principles of Purity, Compassion, Wisdom and Love, they are immortal, and know they are immortal; they are one with God (the Supreme Good), and know they are one with God. Seeing the realities of things, they can find no room anywhere for condemnation. All the operations that occur upon the earth they see as instruments of the Good Law, even those called evil.

All men are essentially divine, though unaware of their divine nature, and all their acts are efforts, even though many of them are dark and impotent, to realize some higher good. All so-called evil is seen to be rooted in ignorance, even those deeds that are called deliberately wicked, so that condemnation ceases, and Love and Compassion become all in all.

But let it not be supposed that the children of the kingdom live in ease and indolence (these two sins are the first that have to be eradicated when the search for the Kingdom is entered upon); they live in a peaceful activity; in fact, they only truly live, for the life of self with its train of worries, griefs, and fears, is not real life.

They perform all their duties with the most scrupulous diligence, apart from thoughts of self, and employ all their means, as well as powers and faculties, which are greatly intensified, in building up the Kingdom of Righteousness in the hearts of others and in the world around them. This is their work—first by example, then by precept.

Having sold all that they have (renounced all self-interest in their possessions), they now give to the poor (give of their rich store of wisdom, love and peace to the needy in spirit, the weary and broken-hearted), and follow the Christ whose name is LOVE.

And they have sorrow no more, but live in perpetual gladness, for though they see suffering in the world, they also see the final Bliss and the Eternal Refuge of Love, to which whosoever is ready may come now, and to which all will come at last.

The children of the Kingdom are known by their life. They manifest the fruits of the Spirit—"love, joy, peace, long-suffering, kindness, goodness, faithfulness, meekness, temperance, self-control"—under all circumstances and vicissitudes. They are entirely free from anger, fear, suspicion, jealousy, caprice, anxiety, and grief. Living in the Righteousness of

God, they manifest qualities which are the very reverse of those which occur in the world, and which are regarded by the world as foolishness.

They demand no rights; they do not defend themselves; do not retaliate; do good to those who attempt to injure them; manifest the same gentle spirit toward those who oppose and attack them as toward those who agree with them; do not pass judgement on others; condemn no person and no system, and live at peace with all.

The Kingdom of Heaven is perfect trust, perfect knowledge, perfect peace. All is music, sweetness, and tranquillity. No irritations, no bad tempers, no harsh words, no suspicions, no lust, and no disturbing elements can enter there.

Its children live in perfect sweetness, forgiving and forgiven, ministering to others with kindly thoughts and words, and deeds. And that Kingdom is in the heart of every man and woman; it is their rightful heritage, their own Kingdom; theirs to enter now. But no sin can enter therein; no self-born thought or deed can pass its Golden Gates; no impure desire can defile its radiant robes.

All may enter it who will, but all must pay the price, and that is—the unconditional abandonment of self.

"If thou wilt be perfect, sell all that thou hast"; but at these words the world turns away "sorrowful, for it is very rich"; rich in money which it cannot keep; rich in fears which it cannot let go; rich in selfish loves to which it greedily clings; rich in grievous partings which it would fain escape; rich in seeking enjoyment; rich in pain and sorrow; rich in strife and suffering; rich in excitement and woe; rich in all things which are not riches, but poor in riches themselves which are not to be found outside the Kingdom; rich in all things that pertain to darkness and death, but poor in those things which are Light and Life.

He then, who would realize the Kingdom, let him pay the price and enter. If he have a great and holy faith he can do it now, and, letting fall from him like a garment the self to which he has been clinging, stand free. If he have less faith, he must rise above self more slowly, and find the Kingdom by daily effort and patient work. The Temple of Righteousness is built and its four walls are the four Principles— Purity, Wisdom, Compassion, Love. Peace is its roof; its floor Steadfastness, its entrance-door is Selfless Duty, its atmosphere is Inspiration, and its music is the Joy of the perfect.

It cannot be shaken, and, being eternal and indestructible, there is no more need to seek protection in taking thought for the things of tomorrow. And the

Kingdom of Heaven being established in the heart,
the obtaining of the material necessities of life is no
more considered, for, having found the Highest, all
these things are added as effect to cause; the struggle
for existence has ceased, and the spiritual, mental,
and material needs are daily supplied from the universal abundance.

Long I sought thee, Spirit holy,
Master Spirit, meek and lowly;
Sought thee with a silent sorrow,
brooding over the woes of men;
Vainly sought thy yoke of meekness
'Neath the weight of woe and weakness;
Finding not, yet in my failing,
seeking over and over again.

In unrest and doubt and sadness
Dwelt I, yet I knew thy Gladness
Waited somewhere; somewhere
greeted torn and sorrowing hearts like mine;
Knew that somehow I should find thee,
Leaving sin and woe behind me,
And at last thy Love would bid me
enter into Rest divine.

Hatred, mockery, and reviling
Scorched my seeking soul defiling
That which should have been thy Temple,
wherein thou shouldest move and dwell;

Praying, striving, hoping, calling;
Suffering, sorrowing in my falling,
Still I sought thee, groping blindly in the
gloomy depths of Hell.

And I sought thee till I found thee;
And the dark powers all around me
Fled, and left me silent, peaceful, brooding
over thy holy themes;
From within me and without me
Fled they when I ceased to doubt thee;
And I found thee in thy Glory, mighty Master
of my dreams!

Yes, I found thee, Spirit holy,
Beautiful and pure and lowly;
Found thy Joy and Peace and Gladness;
found thee in thy House of Rest;
Found thy strength in Love and Meekness,
And my pain and woe and weakness left me,
And I walked the Pathway trodden only by the blest.

Other Titles by
Janice & Mel's
Life Transformation Publishing

As a Man Thinketh
by James Allen

The Way of Peace
by James Allen

The Path of Prosperity
by James Allen

The Mastery of Destiny
by James Allen

The Heavenly Life
by James Allen

Entering the Kingdom
by James Allen

Byways of Blessedness
by James Allen

Printed in Great Britain
by Amazon